The Allied Victory

Sean Sheehan

RAINTREE
STECK-VAUGHN
PUBLISHERS

A Harcourt Company

Austin   New York
www.steck-vaughn.com

THE WORLD WARS

Published by Raintree Steck-Vaughn Publishers,
an imprint of Steck-Vaughn Company

Library of Congress Cataloging-in-Publication Data
Sheehan, Sean.
The Allied Victory / Sean Sheehan.
    p.   cm.—(The World Wars)
  Includes bibliographical references and index.
  ISBN 0-7398-2755-3
  1. World War, 1939–1945—Campaigns—Juvenile literature.
  [1. World War, 1939–1945—Campaigns.] I. Title. II. Series.

  D743 .S44   2001
  940.54'2—dc21   00-062822

Printed in Italy. Bound in the United States.
1 2 3 4 5 6 7 8 9 0 05 04 03 02 01

Acknowledgment for quotes:
Victory poem (quoted on p. 255
of Overy's *Russia's War*.) From
I. Ehrenburg, *Men—Years—Life:
The War 1941–45* (London, 1964,
p. 191); *Beginning and End* poem;
quoted from Norman Davies:
Europe, A History.

Picture acknowledgments:
AKG 14, 17, 20, 25, 31, 32, 33,
42, 43, 50, 53, 56, 59; Camera
Press 9, 15; HWPL cover (inset
right) 26/7, 38, 48; Military
Picture Library cover (inset left);
Peter Newark's Military Pictures
cover (main), 4, 6, 7, 9, 10, 11,
13, 16, 19, 21, 22, 28 (right), 34,
41, 46, 47, 54, 57; Popperfoto 12,
18, 24, 28 (left), 29, 45, 49, 51,
55; Topham 37, 39.
Main cover photograph: British and
Canadian troops advance on a
heavily defended Reichswald forest,
Germany, February 1945. Insets:
(top) the badge of the Allied troops
that took part in the campaign
from the north, the 1st/2nd
British/Commonwealth army and
(lower) the 1st U.S. Air Force.
Map artwork by Peter Bull.

Contents

Germany and Japan halted

Introduction

At the beginning of 1942, World War II turned into a global conflict. Adolf Hitler's occupation of countries in Europe had resulted in a war on different fronts. The British and their allies were fighting the Germans and Italians in North Africa and in the Mediterranean. Meanwhile, Hitler had turned his attention east and invaded the USSR in the second half of 1941, halting at Moscow on December 5. The war became truly global when, in December 1941, Japan invaded British Malaya and attacked the American fleet at Pearl Harbor. This resulted in the immediate entry of the United States and Great Britain into the war against Japan.

The year 1942 became one of fluctuating fortunes for the nations at war, without a decisive blow on either side. The German invasion of the USSR had left more than three million Soviet citizens killed and another three million captured. Hitler was now determined to finish the job. His ambition was to strike south into the Caucasus, with its rich deposits of oil, and knock out the industrial base around the city of Stalingrad. He then aimed to move north to capture Moscow from behind the Russian lines.

The Battle for Stalingrad involved vicious hand-to-hand fighting for control of a piece of road or a building, even for individual rooms in a house.

Paulus's Sixth Army and a panzer division are surrounded at Stalingrad, trapping around 270,000 men. Paulus sent a message to Hitler: "Army heading for disaster. It is essential to withdraw all our divisions from Stalingrad." Hitler refused the request and ordered him to stand firm.

Operation Uranus

Stalingrad was a sprawling mix of homes and industry named after the country's ruler. It stretched for more than 60 miles (60 km) along the banks of the Volga River in the USSR. By August 1942, the invading German Sixth Army under General Friedrich Paulus was on the outskirts of the city, but complete victory for the Germans was proving elusive. The Russians fought in the streets, defending their city, building by building, hiding in the sewers, and suffering greatly. The Russians gambled on a daring counteroffensive, code-named Uranus, which aimed to reach the rear of the enemy line in a pincer movement to cut off the Sixth Army from the rest of the German front.

Unknown to the Germans, the Red Army secretly coordinated a force of more than one million men.

5

The Germans were not prepared for the attack when it was launched on November 19, 1942. By January 1943 the Germans, who were surrounded at Stalingrad, were reeling under the blow of massive bombardments and temperatures of -22 °F (-30 °C), while surviving on food rations of less than 2 ounces (60 g) of bread and .5 ounces (15 g) of sugar a day. The Russians pressed on, with soldiers in the frontline having a life expectancy that could often be measured in hours.

Paulus, who refused to surrender as the ring of tanks and soldiers closed in on his men, finally admitted defeat when his own headquarters were surrounded on the last day of January. Hitler was extremely angry that Paulus allowed himself to be taken alive instead of committing suicide. German losses were catastrophic with well over 100,000 dead. Of the 90,000 Germans taken prisoner, only 5 percent survived if they were ordinary soldiers; although, if they were senior officers, only 5 percent died in captivity.

A famous photograph showing the red flag being waved by a soldier over the smoldering ruins of Stalingrad to signal the Russian victory in January 1943.

A journalist who entered the city in February 1943 described the deserted urban landscape of ruins and frozen bodies as "a fossilized hell, as though a raving

lunatic had suddenly died of heart failure." The modern city of Volgograd, as Stalingrad is now called, was built over the bones of the two million civilians who died in the conflict. Those who managed to survive were close to death from starvation, like three children who were huddled in a bed clinging to one another for warmth when soldiers arrived outside, speaking Russian. One of the children recalled how, "We began to scream, 'Don't kill us! We're Russians!'. . . When they came in and saw us, they burst into tears."

If Stalingrad had been conquered by the Germans, the disaster might have caused a fatal collapse of Soviet morale. It was not to be. The defeat of the German Sixth Army at Stalingrad marked a decisive turning point. Never again would a Nazi army advance deep into Soviet territory. Nevertheless, it was not the end of the war on the Eastern front because the surviving armies hung on tenaciously. It would take another two years of bitter fighting to liberate all of Russia.

An American Stuart tank in North Africa. One soldier who survived the war in the desert said, "Your vehicle was your life, quite literally. We loved our vehicles and we'd do anything to keep them going."

Invasion of North Africa

If the Germans and their allies were ever to be defeated in western Europe, then an invasion of the European continent would have to take place. The Russians hoped that the Allies (the British, Americans, and the other nations supporting them), would mount an invasion in 1942. This would mean that Germany would have to reduce its strength in the east in order to deal with such a threat. The Allies set their sights on 1943 as the earliest possible date to mount such an invasion but, in the meantime, a much smaller-scaled invasion of North Africa (code-named Torch) presented itself as a possibility.

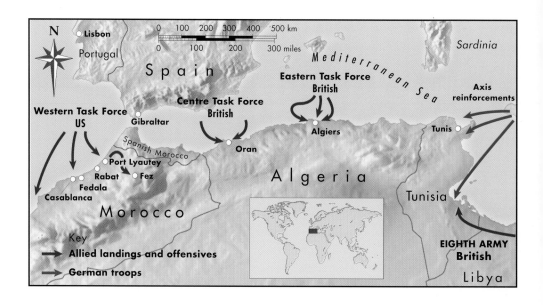

In November 1942, the invasion forces of Operation Torch landed in North Africa. Allied troops swept eastward, although they met with stiff resistance from German forces who were reinforced by an airlift into Tunisia.

North Africa already existed as a theater of war where the Germans and Italians were fighting British and Commonwealth troops in Egypt. In North Africa the Germans had the Suez Canal in their sights, and Hitler's grand design was to link up his armies in the Middle East. But there was to be no decisive victory. In the final months of 1942 a landing of combined American and British troops in Morocco and Algeria was planned to advance eastward toward the Germans, sandwiching them in Tunisia after the British Eighth Army advanced westward from Libya.

The Torch invasion, which began on November 8, 1942, was the first time that a combined force had mounted such an operation. It was not an outright success. The Americans landed too far west at Casablanca and the British, who landed farther east in Algeria, were still some distance from Tunisia. It was February 1943 before the rival armies engaged each other, and the result was again inconclusive. Eventually the Germans were defeated by their lack of oil and food. The Allies had won control in the air, as well as inflicting heavy losses on the Italian navy. By blockading their supply lines, and after heavy fighting, the Germans were forced to surrender in Tunisia on May 13, 1943.

General Bernard Montgomery and his staff meet with the army commanders of the surrendered Italian and German forces in Tunisia. The map is to help set up assembly points for all the captured troops.

The capture of 130,000 Axis troops was a disaster for Germany—the failure was second only to Stalingrad. The Mediterranean was now open to the Allies. On the other hand, this victory had taken five months to achieve and the delay meant it would not be possible to organize an invasion of France in 1943. Instead, plans were made for an invasion of Sicily and then Italy.

Japan halted

The Japanese attack on Pearl Harbor on December 7, 1941 had not delivered the killing blow that was planned. The Japanese admiral, Isoroku Yamamoto, devised a plan to finish off what the Japanese saw as "the American threat" in June 1942. He chose two tiny American-occupied islands called Midway, in the middle of the Pacific Ocean. He knew the United States would want to defend these islands because if they were captured they would provide a base for direct attacks on the west coast of the mainland. Yamamoto planned to invade the islands as a bait, drawing the American aircraft carriers to their defense and then destroying them with his own navy. Yamamoto also planned a decoy, involving the Aleutian Islands, as part of the trap. By invading these islands that lay more than 994 miles (1,600 km) to the north, he hoped that he could split the American forces, who would then have to send ships there to counter the threat.

It was an audacious plan but the stakes were high for, if successful, it would leave the Americans powerless to intervene in Asia. What was not known was that the Japanese naval codes, used to send and receive messages by radio, had been deciphered by the Americans. With full knowledge of the plan, the U.S. was able to ignore the decoy attack on the Aleutian Islands and mount their own surprise attack on the Japanese navy.

The Japanese lost their four largest aircraft carriers and more than 300 ships, marking a decisive point in the Pacific war that was kept secret from the Japanese public. A Japanese officer who was wounded remembered how his presence in the hospital was hushed up: "No nurses or medical attendants were allowed in, and I could not communicate with the world outside. All the wounded from Midway were treated like this. It was like being a prisoner of war among your own people."

It took U.S. planes only minutes to bomb Japanese aircraft carriers in the Battle of Midway, June 1942. The result spelled the beginning of the end for Japanese power in the Pacific.

War in the Pacific

The Battle of Midway was the first irreversible military victory achieved by the Allies in World War II. It was one in a series of battles fought between May 1942 and February 1943 that resulted in the Americans achieving a dominant position in the Pacific. The main battleground lay to the north of Australia, around and on the Solomon Islands and the much larger island of New Guinea.

It was the Solomon island of Guadalcanal that gave its name to a major encounter between American and Japanese forces on land and sea, and in the air. It started in August 1942 when U.S. Marines landed on the island, and ended in February 1943 when the surviving Japanese troops evacuated Guadalcanal. Fighting on land was confined to around 20 sq miles (52 sq km) on the northern coast, but some 50 actions involving warships were carried out.

At the eastern end of New Guinea, Australian troops engaged and broke a Japanese offensive. Australia, sharing with Northern Ireland the distinction of never having introduced conscription, had half its young male population enlisting voluntarily, and nearly 90 percent of all males over 14 were engaged directly in war work.

Below: Some 25,000 Japanese soldiers lost their lives trying to defend the small Pacific island of Guadalcanal against U.S. troops, seen here coming ashore in August 1942.

Strategies for victory

Making decisions

At the beginning of 1943, two Allied leaders, Franklin D. Roosevelt and Winston Churchill, met in Casablanca to discuss future strategies. The third leader, Josef Stalin, was not able to attend because he was preoccupied with the German invasion. Roosevelt and Churchill may have been allies, but there were many areas of disagreement concerning the future conduct of the war.

Roosevelt and Churchill met in Casablanca in January 1943 and put on a united front for the benefit of war correspondents and the American and British public.

The focus of interest for the British was the Mediterranean, for this was their sea link to the oil-rich Middle East as well as to their imperial interests in India. The longer and more dangerous route around South Africa added to the losses being incurred by carrying supplies across the Atlantic. This had the effect of nearly bankrupting Great Britain. The Americans were more interested in an invasion of northern Europe, but they came to accept that this could not take place until 1944, and plans for an invasion of Italy went ahead.

General MacArthur

General MacArthur was one of the most unconventional leaders to achieve fame during World War II. Having escaped the Japanese-occupied Philippines by speedboat in 1942, he swore he would return to the islands. He took charge of Australian forces— whom he inspired with confidence. No other military leader in the war had such a sense of history, and MacArthur would compare his strategy behind the capture of a Pacific atoll with a bygone victory by Napoleon or Hannibal. One of his favorite sayings was, "Nature is neutral in war, but if you beat it, and the enemy does not, it becomes a powerful ally."

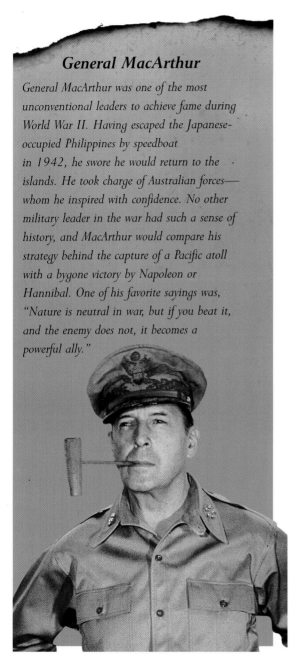

General Douglas MacArthur (1880-1964) often acted in an unconventional way for an army general but remained one of the most popular high-ranking officers of the war.

The growing power of the United States in the conflict in Asia was not disputed by the Allies but there was disagreement about the best strategy to pursue. The United States was not impressed with British efforts to recapture Burma from the Japanese, and attitudes toward the nationalist leader in China, Chiang Kai-shek, differed. Roosevelt's faith in the ability of the Chinese leader to help defeat Japan was not shared by the British. In time, the role of China in the war became less important to the Allies, but this only emerged later and it was not until May 1943 that a strategy for war in the Pacific was agreed to.

America's Pacific war was divided between the navy under Admiral Chester W. Nimitz and the army under General Douglas MacArthur. Rivalry between these two services meant that neither one would submit to being under the command of the other. MacArthur wanted to focus on reconquering the Philippines, where his army had been humiliated in early 1942, while Nimitz favored an island-hopping strategy aimed at reaching Japan but avoiding a confrontation with enemy strongholds in places such as the Philippines, Indonesia, and Singapore. A two-pronged strategy that allowed the two commanders to follow their own policies was a compromise that in the end turned out to be very successful. What was not successful was the debate about bombing Germany into submission from the air.

German cities were heavily bombed toward the end of the war, killing hundreds of thousands of civilians.

The failure of Bomber Harris

British Air Chief Marshal Arthur Harris earned his nickname, "Bomber" Harris, because of his relentless pursuit of a policy of large-scale bombing raids on German towns. Apart from the morality of massacring almost one million citizens, the twin aims of breaking the enemy's morale and destroying industrial production were not successful.

Instead, the Americans wanted to pursue a strategy of bombing selected military and industrial targets while at the same time trying to knock out the German fighter planes that attacked their pilots. Harris was, nevertheless, remarkably successful in pursuing his own agenda, and a combined British and American ten-day bombing mission was launched on Hamburg at the end of July 1943. More than half the city's homes were destroyed and some 45,000 civilians were killed, but the impact on industrial output was minimal. The American policy of precision bombing did not achieve success until the introduction of the U.S.'s long-range fighter plane known as the Mustang.

Dear Mom, Pop

Dear Mom, Pop, Frances, Edith, Marion, Leon, and Aaron:

Am going on a raid this afternoon or early in the morning. There is a possibility I won't return. In any event, please do not worry too much about me as everyone has to leave this earth one way or another...If after this terrible war is over, the world emerges a saner place to live, if all nationalities are treated equal, pogroms and persecution halted, then I'm glad I gave my efforts with thousands of others for such a cause. Wish I had time to write more, but sometimes the less said the better, so goodbye—and good luck—always.
Carl

Letter from an American gunner to his family, February 16, 1943

Invasion of Italy

The island of Sicily, off the southern tip of Italy, was invaded on July 10, 1943, by a massive joint force of 150,000 British and American troops protected by a thousand aircraft. The total number of men that landed eventually swelled to a half million.

While the invasion was taking place, momentous political events were taking place in Italy. Benito Mussolini's government had brought disaster to the country, and the ruling groups that had once supported his seizure of power now conspired to remove him. He was deposed by members of his own party and whisked away as a virtual prisoner. The men who succeeded him began negotiating surrender terms with the Allies while trying to keep this a secret from Germany. Hitler, however, became aware of what was happening and reacted by sending Field Marshal Erwin Rommel into northern Italy with troops. He also sent fresh troops into the south of Italy as reinforcements for his general, Albert Kesselring. Italy was about to surrender, but Hitler had no intention of leaving his back door open for the Allies to move up into Germany.

Allied troops storm and capture a railway station during the first days of the invasion of Sicily in July 1943. Churchill believed that an invasion of Italy would provide a back way into Europe for the Allies.

By early September 1943, when Allied troops were arriving on the southern Italian mainland from Sicily, German troops seized control of Rome. Italy was now split in two, with the Germans in the north controlling two thirds of the country while British and American troops held the south of the country. The Allies, who found their way blocked by a determined German resistance, would take 18 months to capture Rome. It was an advantage for Allied air power to be able to operate from southern Italy, and the invasion had provoked the overthrow of Mussolini and the end of Italian fascism.

The ability of U.S. factories to mass-produce planes, tanks, and weapons was one of the most decisive factors in the ultimate victory of the Allies during World War II.

A booming economy

After the hard times of the Depression, the war years were a boom time for the American war-fueled economy, and more than 17 million new jobs were created. Although there was some rationing, most people had more money to spend than ever before and luxury items were available on the black market. The Coca-Cola empire began with the establishment of overseas bottling plants in response to its success in supplying the armed forces abroad. The average sale in an American department store increased from $2 to $10 in the early 1940s. For most people the war was a faraway event. Their country was not bombed or invaded by the enemy, and the number of those who died in combat was relatively small: More Russians died at Stalingrad than did Americans during the whole of World War II.

Events in Russia

In terms of the eventual defeat of Germany, the tank battle around Kursk in Russia in 1943 was more significant than the strategy of "Bomber" Harris or even the invasion of Italy. Even after their defeat at Stalingrad, the Germans still had military options; but after their defeat at Kursk, with the loss of vital armored formations, the only option left was retreat. The huge drain on German resources and morale brought about by the successive defeats inflicted on the German army in Russia made this the crucial factor in the Allied victory in Europe.

Although committed to a policy of first achieving victory in Europe, by the end of 1943 the United States had more troops, ships, and planes fighting against Japan than against Germany. Most significant was the success achieved by submarines against Japanese merchant and military shipping. By October 1943 the Americans were confident about the ability of their aircraft carriers and warships to support amphibious assaults in the central Pacific.

These soldiers engaged in the Battle of Kursk were part of a vast operation that decisively defeated the Germans and marked a major military turning point in the war in Europe.

The year 1943 drew to a close with another conference of the Allied powers. This time the meeting was at Tehran and all three leaders—Churchill, Roosevelt, and Stalin—met together for the first time. The most momentous decision taken at Tehran was the United States and Great Britain's firm commitment to invade Europe through northern France. This confirmed that the three great powers would support one another until Germany was comprehensively defeated. Hitler's last chance of survival was to hope that the forces allied against him would not hold together. The conference at Tehran finally destroyed that hope and Germany's defeat was now only a matter of time.

Effects of war

- The crime rate in Great Britain rose by 60 percent.
- The number of illegitimate births rose by 40 percent in Great Britain.
- The divorce rate rose by 75 percent in Great Britain.
- In the United States the divorce rate and the number of illegitimate births more than doubled.
- Stealing food carried the death penalty in Russia.
- A loaf of bread cost almost a week's wages on the black market in Russia.

By the time Stalin, Roosevelt, and Churchill met for the Tehran Conference in December 1943, the Russians were probably strong enough to defeat Nazi Germany on their own.

The struggle for Europe

Mistakes in Italy

The invasion of Italy in 1943 was not a disaster but neither did it prove particularly successful. The Germans were still holding the north of the country and had a defensive line, called the Gustav Line, in the mountains south of Rome. Churchill persuaded the Americans to land Allied forces at Anzio in January 1944, on the coast south of Rome though behind the German defensive line. This advantage was lost by poor generalship and, instead, the troops at Anzio found themselves trapped. In Churchill's words, "We would be hurling a wildcat ashore, but all we got was a stranded whale."

U.S. troops board landing craft for the amphibious assault at Anzio. The landing was unopposed by the Germans, but the commander failed to make good use of the situation and nothing of consequence was achieved.

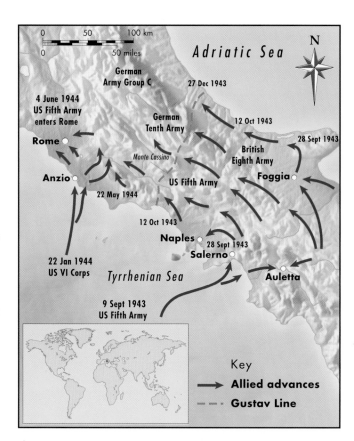

By the end of September 1943, the Allies had got ashore in Italy and had moved as far north as Naples. By November, General Montgomery's Eighth Army had started its assault on the Gustav Line. The landings at Anzio in January 1944 took the Germans by surprise, but counterattacks stopped the Allies short of Monte Cassino. The capital, Rome, was not secured by U.S. forces until June 1944.

The attack that destroyed the monastery at Monte Cassino on February 15, 1944, remains controversial. One of the generals in charge later regretted the operation.

The Germans eventually withdrew farther north and established another defensive line, but instead of pursuing them, the commander at Anzio preferred to capture Rome. It was a symbolic rather than a strategic victory. Underlying some of the difficulties was the difference of opinion between the British and Americans

over the best way to invade Europe. Breaking through the Gustav Line also revealed inadequacies in the Allied command, and the German general, Kesselring, proved more farsighted and competent.

Monte Cassino

Monte Cassino was a sixth-century Benedictine monastery built on a large rock on the Gustav Line. Allied commanders convinced themselves it was being used as a German observation post to direct the devastating accuracy of enemy fire. After men of 15 nationalities failed to reach it, around 500 tons of bombs were dropped from planes and the abbey was totally destroyed. The Nazis had agreed with the Vatican that they would not use it and, fortunately, had already removed its priceless art treasures. The rubble and ruins provided excellent cover for the Germans and only served to strengthen their defensive position.

Russians advance westward

There were now more than three million Axis soldiers in the east facing more than six million of the enemy. They were similarly outnumbered in tanks and planes. What the Germans lacked in numbers they made up for in terms of quality weapons, experience, and a grim determination not to allow a vengeful enemy to invade their country. Knowledge of their own behavior and attitude when invading the USSR could give them no illusions about how they might expect to be treated if positions were to be reversed.

This painting of the ruined abbey of Monte Cassino captures the sense of waste and destruction brought about by war.

At the beginning of 1944, Leningrad in the north of the USSR was freed from the ordeal of a prolonged siege that saw one million civilians starve to death. The German army still stood firm in the center, in what is now Belarus. In June, the Soviet army moved against them in a major offensive code-named Operation Bagration. Like their allies in the west who were preparing to invade France, they managed to prevent the Germans from knowing where their attack would come from. The Germans anticipated an attack from the south, where the bulk of the Soviet armored divisions were stationed, and elaborate measures were taken to confirm this impression. Dummy forces were set up in the south and defensive fortifications were created to create the illusion that the Russians were now resting after nearly a year of continuous combat. A high degree of secrecy was maintained about the Soviet attack up until the last moment. Even the drivers of the trains transporting the troops were unaware of their destination.

The attack began on June 10 with a feint attack into Finland in the north, while the operation opened in Belarus on June 22, the anniversary of the German invasion of Russia. The attack was an overwhelming

Stubborn fighting by armed resistance in Leningrad meant that the invitations printed in Berlin for an official victory party, with Hitler as guest of honor, were never mailed.

Women fighters

Russian women fought against the Germans in 1944 in both the air force and army. There was an entire women's regiment, the 46th Guards Women's Night Light-Bomber Regiment, that used biplanes with open cockpits and had their own female mechanics. Combat troops on the ground included more than a quarter million women by 1945.

By the end of July 1944, the Russians were closing in on Warsaw, having liberated cities such as Minsk before reaching Poland. However, German resistance stiffened as they approached the capital. The Poles saw their chance to rise up against their German occupiers in Warsaw, but their uprising proved a tragic disaster and the city was razed to the ground.

success, taking the Germans completely by surprise and capturing 400,000 prisoners. Soviet forces in the south of the USSR had not even been used, and early in July Stalin gave the order to move toward Warsaw, the capital of Poland. By July 25 the Russians had reached the capital and only now did determined German resistance hold them back. The Poles, thinking their chance had at last arrived, rose in revolt in Warsaw.

The Warsaw uprising

The Warsaw uprising began on the first day of August 1944. Despite initial successes, the Poles were handicapped by a lack of heavy weapons against an enemy that was given orders to destroy the city and everyone in it. About 225,000 civilians died in what was the single largest atrocity in the history of the war. People were massacred by the thousands while trying to escape the bloodbath. After two months of fierce fighting, the rebels surrendered and the remaining civilian population was transported to German death camps. What was left of the city was then systematically razed to the ground, and it took three months to fulfill Hitler's order that not a single building should be left standing.

The uprising was an attempt by Polish nationalists to liberate the city from the Germans before the Russians could gain control over their capital. At the city gates, the Russians were unable to break through the defensive measures taken by the Germans, who knew that the

Some 10,000 Polish soldiers, seen here dislodging Germans from their positions in the suburbs of Warsaw, died in their failed uprising. When the fighting ended at the beginning of October 1944, the city and its people suffered even more.

gateway to Berlin would be open once Warsaw fell to the enemy. After a sustained lull in the operations, the Red Army mounted another major offensive in January 1945 that carried it from Warsaw to the gates of Berlin.

In August 1944, the remaining German army in the north of Romania was defeated, with 400,000 prisoners taken. The Soviet Red Army swept into Bulgaria and Yugoslavia and, by the end of 1944, the capital of Hungary was under siege. Stalin, who in 1943 had been on the defensive deep within his own country, was now master of large parts of eastern Europe.

Operation Overlord

The invasion of northwest Europe, code-named Overlord, involved an astonishing degree of planning. An enormous amount of military hardware was transported to Normandy, including two artificial harbors that were towed across the sea to facilitate the landings. Specially adapted tanks, such as the Sherman which could be driven through the water by a propeller attached to its rear, worked better in theory than in practice. Another tank, the Churchill carpet layer, was fitted with an attachment at the front that laid down a track over boggy land. Pluto (Pipeline Under the Ocean), which provided a continuous supply of gasoline, was not an immediate success. General Dwight D. Eisenhower, in overall command of the operation, humorously remarked that, "Only the great number of barrage balloons floating constantly in British skies [to deter enemy planes] kept the islands from sinking under the waves."

An Allied tank rolls off its transport plane as part of the preparations for Operation Overlord, the invasion of northwest Europe in June 1944.

D-Day

The long-delayed invasion of northern Europe finally took place on June 6, 1944, weeks before the Russians launched their surprise attack on the Germans. In both campaigns, elaborate and successful precautions were taken to create the vital element of surprise. A phantom force was set up on the English south coast opposite Calais, with a flurry of activity on the ground and in the air to give the impression that this would be the direction of the invasion. Hitler and his general, Rommel, both correctly guessed that Normandy was the likely landing place, but Hitler hedged his bets by equally dividing his forces between the Normandy and Calais areas.

Germany had the more general problem of trying to prepare for two offensives, one from the east and one from the west. Large numbers of troops and equipment waited in the east, and of the 58 divisions in the west, only 15 were in Normandy, where the Allies actually landed. The Germans perceived that the greatest danger lay on the eastern front.

D-Day began in the middle of the night with American paratroopers jumping into the middle of enemy lines. One of them, a young man from Kansas, found himself

suspended from the spire of the Sainte-Mère church but survived by pretending to be dead. The first British soldier landed his glider but was knocked unconscious on impact. By the end of that day, some 150,000 soldiers had come ashore on to five code-named beaches in a remarkable organizational success.

However, not everything went according to plan. The American units that landed on Omaha beach suffered heavy casualties. The British were unable to capture Caen, and the Americans took three weeks to take the principal port of Cherbourg. On the other hand, the Allies had the enormous advantage of overwhelming air superiority; some 10,000 Allied aircraft were faced by only 500 German aircraft. The Allies had been able to cross the Channel without opposition, and their air power also wreaked havoc on German supply lines and transport routes across France. By September, there were about two

D-Day Diary

June 6: 6 A.M. Sea very rough. Hit the beach at 7:20 A.M. Murderous fire, losses high. I was lucky....Terrible fighting and ghastly sights.

June 7: Still going. Dug in at 2 A.M. Away again at 5:30 A.M. No food. Going into another village: Sgt lost.

June 8: 7:30 A.M. Fire coming from village. Village cleared. Prisoners taken. German snipers lurking in wood. Had two hours sleep. Second rest since the 6th.

June 9: 6:00 A.M. Carried on wood clearing. Germans flown. Only one killed for our morning's work. We are now about 8 to 10 miles inland. Promoted to Sgt.

June 10: Joan darling, I have not had you out of my thoughts....We have lost some good men....The French people have given us a good welcome. Had wine.

June 11: Contact with enemy. Lost three of my platoon.

Adapted from the diary of G.E. Hughes, who took part in the invasion of Normandy

The invasion of France began just before dawn on June 6 and 200,000 men were involved on the first day in naval operations. Some landings proceeded as planned; others went very wrong.

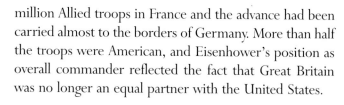

General Eisenhower, in overall charge of the D-Day invasion of Europe, had prepared a statement accepting responsibility in case the invasion was a failure.

million Allied troops in France and the advance had been carried almost to the borders of Germany. More than half the troops were American, and Eisenhower's position as overall commander reflected the fact that Great Britain was no longer an equal partner with the United States.

There was disagreement between the commanders over the best way to advance. Eisenhower felt he could not allow the British Army Group to push too far ahead at the risk of eclipsing the American forces who also wanted the glory of pushing into Germany.

The year 1944 drew to a close with the Germans mounting a counteroffensive that exposed weaknesses in Allied generalship but that ultimately failed. It was now the turn of the Allies to be taken by surprise, for they ignored signs of enemy preparations for an attack, thinking the Germans were no longer able to mount an offensive. The attack, which began in December with infiltrators in American uniforms and jeeps cutting lines of communication, was a warning that Hitler had no intention of surrendering.

French civilians welcome advancing Allied soldiers as they cross a bridge over the River Seine. Thousands of men like these would die before the Germans finally retreated from northern France.

Partisans and resistance

Partisans, the name given to guerrilla groups fighting German forces, organized resistance to the Nazis across the length and breadth of Europe. In 1944, they met with varying degrees of success. The uprising in Warsaw was a courageous act but ended in disastrous failure, while in Russia partisans were used systematically and very effectively behind German lines. In Denmark, which was neutral but occupied, the prewar government was still functioning. A general strike was organized by resistance groups and it was so successful that the Germans arrested the entire police force and deported its officers, to Germany.

In France, the ability of resistance groups to fight the enemy was underestimated by the Allied military professionals, who tended to look down on them as amateurs. In reality, they were remarkably effective and could have been brought into the planning of D-Day at an earlier stage.

A photograph taken by a French resistance unit to show how they played their part in helping to ensure the success of the Allied landings.

Many of the partisans in France and Italy were communists and socialists, and they were distrusted by the Allied governments. The governments feared that the partisans would use their success to promote social and political revolution in the wake of helping to defeat the Germans. This is what happened in Yugoslavia, where the partisans were highly organized and played an important military role in helping to defeat the Germans. In Greece also, communist partisans threatened to take control of the country and the British sent in troops to fight them and ensure that a non-communist government took power.

In Germany itself, it was very difficult to organize resistance, mainly because Hitler's authoritarian government had systematically eliminated political opposition in the years before the outbreak of war. This did not completely prevent the development of some underground groups, made up of a mixture of communists, disgruntled generals, and conservative politicians, and there was an attempt on Hitler's life in 1944.

Attempt to kill Hitler

General von Stauffenberg was the only conspirator able to get close enough to Hitler to attempt an assassination. On July 20, 1944, he succeeded in placing a bomb, inside a leather case, in a hut where Hitler was holding a conference. The bomb exploded and Stauffenberg telephoned his associates to say that Hitler was dead. The associates then revealed themselves, thinking the plot, had succeeded.

What had actually happened was that the German leader had been shielded from the force of the bomb by a heavy oak table and only received minor injuries, though four others were killed. Stauffenberg was executed the same day and many associates were later tortured to death and filmed for Hitler's enjoyment. Rommel was implicated in the plot and committed suicide after his family was threatened.

Winning back Asia

Japan's weakness

The Battle of Midway had halted the Japanese but they were still in a powerful position. Their new empire in the east provided them with 80 percent of the world's rubber, over half the world's tin, huge amounts of oil, and plenty of iron. What they lacked was America's ability to apply industrial capitalism to the task of war, and by the beginning of 1944, this had become a grave weakness. By March 1944, one new aircraft was being built every 294 seconds in the United States. The country had 22 new aircraft carriers under construction in 1943 while the Japanese had only three. There were similar inequalities in the numbers of aircraft, submarines, and other warships.

Losses to Japanese merchant shipping were not replaced at a sufficient rate, and Japan found itself unable to transport its valuable economic resources, especially oil, to where they were needed. Japan had also failed to make the best use of its new empire, called the Greater East Asia Co-Prosperity Sphere. There was a failure to build up loyalty in nations that had been colonized and exploited by the British, Dutch, and French before the war. The opportunity to build a new Asian identity was spoken about but not put into practice and the Japanese became, and were seen as, the new masters who simply replaced those they had driven out in 1942.

The difficulties Japan was experiencing were not known to the Allies, and plans went ahead for a land battle with the Japanese army in China as a prelude to landing in Japan itself. The British were charged with the task of breaking through Burma and, in February 1944, the Japanese tried to forestall this by invading India. They encircled the British at Imphal and advanced on Kohima. Under General William Joseph Slim, regarded as the most able British commander during the whole war, the Japanese were soundly defeated.

Japanese soldiers engaged in the battle for Kohima found themselves facing a determined Anglo-Asian army. British, Indian, and Nepalese Gurkha troops fought alongside one another.

31

American troops prepare to land on the Marshall Islands early in 1944. Many of these soldiers had not experienced combat before but harsh training in North and South Carolina had helped to prepare them.

American victories

It was American successes in the Pacific that made China less and less important to the Allies. At the end of January 1944, the Marshall Islands were attacked, then a Japanese base in the Carolines, followed by the loss in June of more than 200 Japanese aircraft in what was called the "Great Marianas Turkey Shoot" in the Battle of the Philippine Sea.

In June 1944, the largest operation yet by the U.S. Navy was put into practice. Using 500 ships, nearly 70,000 men were put ashore on the island of Saipan. The strategic importance of the island made this a crucial battle. If captured, the Americans could use it to bomb Tokyo. Japanese resistance was determined and uncompromising, and perhaps best expressed by their admiral, who told his men, "The fate of the Empire rests on this one battle." It was a battle they lost, but only after the 32,000-strong force on the island died almost to the last man, partly inspired perhaps by the ritual suicide of their commanding general before their final attack. More than 20,000 Japanese civilians on the island also killed themselves, many by throwing themselves over cliff tops.

When news of Saipan began to circulate, the people of Japan began to realize they were losing the war. The resignation of General Hideki Tojo, the effective head of the country's military government, signaled the unease that was also being felt at the highest levels of command.

After Saipan, the Americans pushed on, ahead of their own schedule for advancing against the enemy. When Guam was captured in August, for the first time around 12,000 Japanese surrendered.

A family on the Pacific island of Saipan is discovered by a U.S. Marine in 1944.

"Lighter than a feather"

Recruits to the Japanese army were subject to an intense indoctrination that taught them to regard defeat and capture as the ultimate dishonor. Some wives even killed their children and committed suicide so that their husbands would have no reason to be afraid of dying for their emperor.

"You men have got to be fully in the picture as to what the present position is. Regarding death as something lighter than a feather you men must tackle the task of capturing Imphal. You must accept that the division will be almost annihilated. I have confidence in your courage but should any delinquency occur, I shall take the necessary action. In order to keep the honor of his unit bright, a commander may have to use his sword as a weapon of punishment, shameful though it is to have to shed one's own soldiers' blood on the battlefield."

From a captured battle order in India, 1944

Japanese kamikaze pilots provoked an understandable alarm among Americans. They knew they were powerless against pilots like these who deliberately flew their planes to crash and explode on the decks of ships.

Further success in the Pacific

In October 1944, the Americans began to land on the small island of Leyte in the Philippines. What followed was a large-scale battle at sea, involving more warships than any other naval encounter in history. The Japanese air force had already been seriously weakened, so this time the Japanese gambled on using their fleet of battleships to isolate the American army by luring away their supporting ships with a decoy force.

The plan went very wrong, and there were communication problems on both sides. Japanese ships were sunk by technically weaker warships, including some that had previously been sunk at Pearl Harbor but had been resurrected from the seabed and repaired. The Japanese navy was virtually destroyed at the Battle of Leyte Gulf. This battle was also the first occasion when the Japanese used kamikaze pilots.

The major events in the Pacific from 1943 to August 1945. The maps shows the Allied campaign across the Pacific toward Japan.

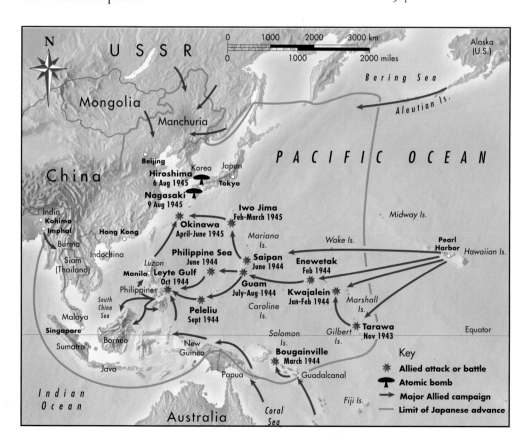

The war in Asia was mostly an American operation, but as the European war drew to a close, the British were anxious to try and reassert their presence in Southeast Asia. They were well aware that the Japanese had shattered the myth of the invincibility of the white man, and that this had seriously undermined the British Empire. In the second half of 1944, a new British Pacific Fleet was ready for action and succeeded in knocking out the two largest Japanese oil refineries at Palembang, in what is, now Indonesia, in January 1945.

Although the new British Pacific Fleet was the largest naval force the British had ever put together, its size was not that impressive compared to the vast assemblage of warships that the United States had built up after Pearl Harbor. Reflecting the fact that the British were now playing second fiddle to the United States in the conduct of the war, overall command for the British navy belonged to American commanders.

The tides of war

I hope everyone at home is fine even though we are all in the midst of this big war. Did Tako evacuate to the countryside with her school friends? Did she go to Hiaki alone? Because of my constant awareness of the tides of war, no single day has ever passed without anxiety and tension....

Although I am not certain about the best place to evacuate to around Tokyo, it seems most likely that Tokyo will be subject to daily air raids within a month or so after our place here is invaded by the enemy. The best place for you to evacuate to seems to be Shinshyu....

I am sending you my battlefield allowance for the months of June and July. I have heard you would get them after September, though I am not certain if I will still be alive....

From General Tadamichi Kuribayshi, on Iwo Jima, to his wife, August 2, 1944.

India's two armies

India had been campaigning for independence before war erupted in Europe in 1939. When it seemed likely that the Japanese would invade the country, the British government tried to win over Mahatma Gandhi, the nationalist leader, with the promise of limited independence once the war was over. But the Indian people wanted full independence, and when a campaign of civil disobedience started, the British imprisoned Gandhi and other leaders.

Indian soldiers, such as these members of a division photographed in May 1944, made up the largest group of volunteers that participated in World War II.

Hundreds of thousands of Indians took part in the war—from Dunkirk to Malaya and Singapore. However, many Indians in Asia found their loyalty to the Allied cause being tested when they experienced the kind of racism that, in 1941, saw the British in Singapore objecting to Indian officers using a club swimming pool.

About 70,000 Indian soldiers were taken prisoner after the fall of Singapore, and the Japanese encouraged them to join the Indian National Army and fight on their side. Chandras Bose, the nationalist leader who led the campaign to free India by joining forces with Japan, had plans to lead this army into India. He imagined they would be triumphant and gain massive support from the people of India.

As it turned out, the Japanese and the Indian National Army were heavily defeated at Imphal and Kohima, and some 35,000 Indians who had changed sides in Singapore now found themselves prisoners of war for the second time, though this time captured by the British.

Mahatma Gandhi, the Indian nationalist leader, was a pacifist, but he condemned Hitler and his policies and expressed moral support for the Allies.

The death railway

Shortly after their 1942 conquests, the Japanese, fearing a blockade by sea, decided to build a railway supply line between Thailand and Burma. As many as 200,000 Asians and 60,000 Allied prisoners of war were used as slave labor. Work began at both ends of the planned railway line in June 1942, and the line was completed by September of the following year. More than 100,000 men died building the railway, roughly one life for every sleeper laid on the track. The Samurai code that governed Japanese military life regarded a man who allowed himself to be taken prisoner as without honor and not worthy of being treated as a human. Forced to work 18-hour shifts, without proper food or medicine, men were worked to death and died from disease and sheer exhaustion.

Japanese engineers estimated that it would take five years to link Burma and Thailand by rail, but prisoners such as these were forced to complete the 250.8 mile (418-km) railway in 16 months.

Final victory

Defeat of Germany

The year 1945 began with Hitler's armies sandwiched between two advancing forces: the Americans, British, and other Allies in the west, and the Russians in the east. Final victory by the Allies now seemed inevitable but Hitler was determined to resist. He hoped that the unlikely alliance between the capitalist west and the communist east would fracture and fall apart.

If this happened, then it was possible that one of the two sides would offer to make separate terms with Germany. By making a deal with one side against the other, some kind of future for Nazism might be possible. Hitler only accepted defeat when it became obvious that the alliance against him would hold firm. Four months of vicious fighting and the loss of many hundreds of thousands of lives was the price paid before Hitler committed suicide in Berlin in April 1945.

A soldier's last words

A reporter asked a group of battle-weary soldiers in Europe, "What would you like best from the States about now?" There was silence until one of them answered: "I've got something to say. Tell them it's too damned serious over here to be talking about hot dogs and baked beans and things we're missing. Tell them. . . there are men getting killed and wounded every minute, and they're miserable and they're suffering. Tell them it's a matter more serious than they'll ever be able to understand. Tell 'em it's rough as hell. Tell 'em it's rough. Tell 'em it's rough, serious business. That's all. That's all."

From *Company Commander*, Charles B. MacDonald (New York, 1947, p. 246). Quoted in *Wartime*, Paul Fussell (Oxford, 1989)

The bombing of Dresden served no military purpose and seemed to be only an act of revenge. Churchill came to question the value of carpet bombing, for "otherwise we shall come into control of an utterly ruined land."

In the western theater of war, the stiff resistance of the Germans led to a renewal of Allied bombing and "Bomber" Harris argued successfully for another massive attack on a German city. Over two days in February, more than a thousand planes destroyed the city of Dresden, creating another firestorm that engulfed the city and killed around 25,000 civilians.

The Allies assembled to the west, while the Russians converged to the east of Berlin, encircling the capital completely by April 25, 1945. The battle for Berlin was completed when the Red Flag was raised on April 30, 1945.

The final Soviet assault on Berlin began on April 26, 1945 and the German Ninth Army made a determined attempt to resist amid the ruins. Some German units were still fighting after Hitler had committed suicide.

Japanese Americans were not allowed to take part in the Pacific war but, in April 1945, they became the first Allied troops to cross into France from the poorly managed invasion of Italy that had begun back in September 1943. The same month also saw a dramatic meeting between American and Russian troops in Germany. When Stalin gave the order for the final advance on Berlin, the Oder River was crossed at night using artificial moonlight created by the reflected beams of searchlights directed at the clouds.

The Russians lost well over 300,000 soldiers in the final, ferocious battle for Berlin, and around the same number of German soldiers and civilians probably died in this final chapter of the war in Europe. It drew to a close when a German general who spoke some Russian appeared with a white flag amid the rubble of Berlin and addressed a Russian general: "Today is the first day of May, a great holiday for our two nations". The Russian dealt coolly with this astonishing act of bravado with the words, "We have a great holiday today. How things are with you over there is less easy to say." The formal act of unconditional surrender was signed on May 7, at Rheims, by General Alfred Jodl. World War II was over in Europe.

On May 7, 1945, Jodl signed an unconditional surrender at Rheims. The next day there was a repeat of the ceremony at the Russian headquarters.

Hitler's last days

On April 29, 1945, nine days after Hitler's 56th birthday, the Russians were so close to the bunker in Berlin where the German leader was holed up that the sound of firing could be heard in the distance. In a bizarre act of matrimony, he married Eva Braun, wrote his last anti-Semitic testament, and the following day committed suicide by shooting himself after swallowing cyanide. His body, along with that of Eva Braun, who had also taken cyanide and died, was taken outside the bunker and set alight after being soaked in gasoline. The day after, Joseph Goebbels (Hitler's propaganda minister) and his wife also committed suicide, having first killed their six children.

1. Lieutenant General Sir F. E. Morgan, Assistant Chief-of-Staff
2. General François Sevez of France
3. Admiral Sir Harold Burrough, Commander of Allied Naval Forces
4. Lieutenant General Walter Bedell Smith, Allied Chief-of-Staff
5. Lieutenant General Ivan Chermiaeff of Russia
6. General Ivan Suslaparov of Russia
7. Lieutenant General Carl Spaatz, Commander of U.S. Strategic Air Forces
8. Major General H.R.Bull, Assistant Chief-of-Staff Operations
9. Lieutenant General Ivan Zemcovitch, aide to Suslaparov
10. Major General Wilhelm Oxenius, aide to Jodl
11. Colonel General Alfred Jodl, German Chief-of-Staff
12. General Admiral Hans G. von Friedeberg, Commander-in-Chief, German navy

Beginning and End

After every war
someone has to clear up.
For things won't find their right place
on their own.

Someone has to heave
the rubble to the roadsides
so the carts piled high with corpses
can pass by.

Photogenic it certainly isn't;
and it takes years.
All the cameras have gone off
to other wars.

Those who knew
what this was all about
must make way for those
who know little, or less than a little,
or simply nothing.

Wislawa Szymborska from
Koniec I początek

(*Beginning and End*, translated from
Polish)

*The Americans thought it would take four days
before they could fly their flag over the volcanic
island of Iwo Jima. In fact, it took many weeks
of heavy and bitter fighting.*

Iwo Jima and Okinawa

The capture of two Pacific islands, Iwo
Jima and Okinawa, in the first half of 1945
represented a tightening of the noose
around Japan. Their capture signaled the
end of Japan's ability to withstand the
military might of the United States. The
8 sq miles (20 sq km) that made up Iwo
Jima was defended, trench by trench, by
20,000 Japanese soldiers who had dug in
with the intention of fighting to the death.
More than 25,000 Americans were killed
before the island was cleared in March, and its strategic
value was put to immediate use when B-29
Superfortresses landed on an emergency runway.
Eventually, half the island became one giant airport from
where bombing raids on Japan were launched.

The campaign to capture Okinawa began on the first
day of April, and it lasted nearly three months.
When the island was finally captured, Americans were

able to use Okinawa as a safe anchorage from which to blockade the Japanese mainland and prevent any supplies from reaching the country. As with Saipan, the island of Okinawa was bitterly defended by the Japanese, who had prepared their positions on the island and employed kamikaze attacks on enemy ships. More than 100,000 Japanese were killed before the island was cleared, but it required a mammoth amount of military hardware to accomplish the task. Over 90,000 missions were flown by American aircraft in the course of the Okinawa campaign, and more gasoline and oil was used up than Japan imported for the whole of the previous year. Together, the two islands cost more American lives than the D-Day invasion of Normandy.

"The greatest thing in history"

While the war in Europe was drawing to a close, the Americans were pondering how best to bring the war in Asia to an end. The losses incurred in the capture of Iwo Jima and

A reef is dynamited near Okinawa in the Pacific in order to provide a landing place for supply ships. Five days after the capture of the island, the Allies called for the surrender of Japan or face "prompt and utter destruction."

Okinawa made the task of a military conquest of the Japanese mainland seem daunting indeed. Although the Japanese were not in a position to win, the Americans did not immediately know how seriously weakened was the enemy. In fact, Japan was on her knees and close to collapse, with two-thirds of her commercial fleet at the bottom of the sea and severe shortages of food and raw materials.

The B-29 Superfortresses were now able to bomb Japanese cities, and in one single raid on a residential area of southern Tokyo in March 1945, more than 80,000 people were killed. What was also likely to accelerate the end of the conflict was Russia's agreement to join the war against Japan within months of defeating Germany. At first, the United States was anxious to encourage this because it promised to hasten the end of the war and save American lives.

U.S. bombing raids on Japan using the B-29 Superfortress had devastating effects and, by the end of June 1945, Japan's war industry was effectively destroyed. The first indications that the country might surrender were made in July.

The B-29 Superfortress

The B-29 Superfortress was an aircraft designed and built for the purpose of mass destruction from the air. The planes were first ready to fly by the middle of 1944 and were used to bomb selected targets in Japan before the end of the year, but with very little success. Then, instead of deploying conventional bombs, the B-29s were used to drop incendiaries (fire bombs). The use of incendiaries on the densely packed streets of Japanese cities, where most homes were built of wood, was catastrophic. When the B-29s took off on a large-scale firebombing of Tokyo, the planes were stripped of most of their defensive armaments to increase the quantity of incendiaries they could carry. The raid lasted more than two hours. It took nearly three weeks to bury the dead, and a million people were left homeless.

By early August, when the collapse of Japan seemed more likely and atom bombs were ready to use, America's attitude toward Russia changed. The United States now preferred to try and bring the war to an end on its own. By this time, Russia wanted to join in the Pacific war and receive its share of the spoils.

Toward the end of July, the Potsdam Declaration, which did not involve Russia, called upon Japan to surrender unconditionally or face complete and immediate destruction. At this stage, there was no assurance that the monarchy and the emperor would escape punishment. Nor were the Japanese aware of their enemy's secret weapon.

America's secret weapon was the successful development of atom bombs, the result of a project that had been focused for three years on the task of controlling a nuclear explosion. Bombs were ready by the middle of 1945 and, after a successful test in New Mexico in July, an atomic bomb was dropped on the city of Hiroshima on August 6. The plane was blessed by a priest before it took off with its deadly cargo.

More than 70,000 civilians were killed almost immediately, and many thousands died later from burns and forms of cancer. Roosevelt had died earlier in the year, and when President Harry Truman received the news of Hiroshima, he exclaimed, "This is the greatest thing in history." A second bomb was later dropped on the city of Nagasaki, with equally horrific consequences.

A mushroom cloud over the city of Hiroshima signaled the dropping of an atomic bomb from a B-29 Superfortress named the Enola Gay. *The chief pilot said he could only see "a black boiling debris down below."*

Emperor Hirohito (1901–89) played an important role in the surrender of Japan, but details of the circumstances surrounding the act of surrender continue to emerge and the full story has yet to be told.

Enduring the unendurable

Japan's surrender was announced by emperor Hirohito when he broadcast by radio to his people that "the unendurable must be endured." The dropping of the atom bombs and the circumstances around the surrender of Japan have remained a controversial topic ever since World War II came to an end.

The Japanese government was split between hardline military leaders, who wanted to fight the Americans on Japanese soil and then negotiate for better surrender terms, and another larger group who saw the hopelessness of the situation and were anxious to make peace. Peace proposals were made to Russia, which were intercepted and read by the United States, but they came to nothing. Even after the Hiroshima bomb, some military leaders were only prepared to call a ceasefire if the Allies promised not to occupy Japan.

It was the emperor who settled the matter by insisting on surrender, having received an assurance from the Americans that the monarchy would not be dismantled by the victors. This assurance was never stated in so many words, but the American statement, made through the neutral Swiss government, that the future government of Japan would be chosen by "the freely expressed will of the Japanese people" amounted to the same thing.

At the last moment, before the emperor made his radio broadcast, a small group of militarists tried to seize the imperial palace and prevent the broadcast from being

committed suicide, preferring death to what they saw as a deep dishonor. The main, formal surrender took place in Tokyo Bay on September 2, 1945. In total, more than 20 million Japanese people were killed, injured, or made homeless during the war. World War II was over in Asia.

General MacArthur is being saluted after the formal surrender of Japan is signed aboard the U.S. battleship Missouri. World War II had finally come to an end.

Unheroic facts

Desertion from the army: About 100,000 cases of desertion occurred in the British army and a similar rate applied to the U.S. army, mostly among infantry troops who experienced the trauma of combat.

Military trials: The United States charged 1.7 million men with breaches of discipline and 142 were executed. More than 200,000 courtmartials took place in the British army.

Avoiding air combat: As many as 25 percent of the planes in some RAF (Royal Air Force) squadrons returned early from raids over Germany, claiming unlikely technical faults. Similar events occurred in the U.S. Army Air Force (USAAF). Deliberately landing in a neutral country where crews were interned as prisoners also took place.

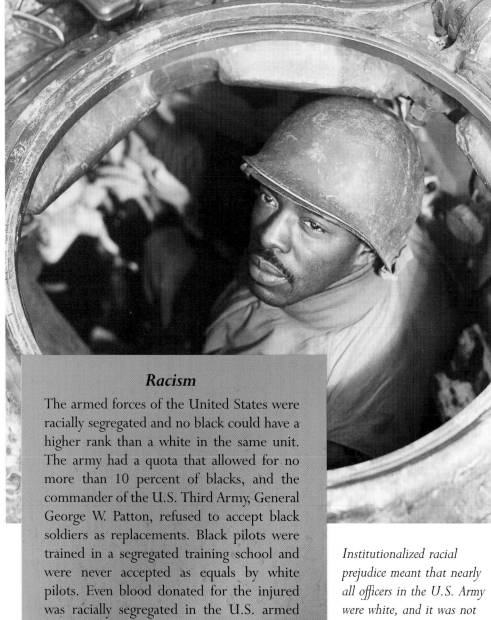

Racism

The armed forces of the United States were racially segregated and no black could have a higher rank than a white in the same unit. The army had a quota that allowed for no more than 10 percent of blacks, and the commander of the U.S. Third Army, General George W. Patton, refused to accept black soldiers as replacements. Black pilots were trained in a segregated training school and were never accepted as equals by white pilots. Even blood donated for the injured was racially segregated in the U.S. armed forces. Authorities in Great Britain and Australia objected to black servicemen being stationed in their countries, but they were generally welcomed by ordinary people. This in turn annoyed authorities in the U.S. Army.

Institutionalized racial prejudice meant that nearly all officers in the U.S. Army were white, and it was not until March 1944 that the U.S. Army allowed black units to be used in combat situations.

Consequences and controversies

Consequences

When World War II came to an end in 1945, the world was a very different place. When the number of those who died as a result of starvation and illness because of war is included, as many as 80 million people had lost their lives. Millions more were homeless, and untold numbers of families were refugees, uprooted from their countries and cultures and forced to try and pick up the pieces of their shattered lives in foreign lands. The pain and suffering of all this would be terrible enough on its own, but there were other consequences, some more far-reaching. The results of World War II have shaped the lives of the generations that followed.

Millions suffered the consequences of war. Amid the ruins of a village on the Eastern front, a Red Army soldier talks to a young boy whose parents were taken by retreating Nazis. He needs crutches because of his frostbitten foot.

The human cost

	Civilian	Combatants
Russia	20 million	8 million
Poland	5 million	120,000
Germany	750,000	3,500,000
Yugoslavia	1.2 million	300,000
Japan	1 million	600,000
Great Britain	100,000	250,000
U.S.A.		300,000
Jews	6 million (Holocaust)	

The war unleashed a level of barbarity and violence that is hard to square with the idea of ourselves as civilized people. Ordinary men and women killed and maimed other ordinary men and women—and while atrocities were committed on both sides, there was nothing to match the horror of the Holocaust.

Even the battle-wearied soldiers who swept across conquered Europe in 1945 were shocked, and some were traumatized, when they entered the German death camps. Using modern industrial technology, the Nazis had built and maintained large camps to receive Jews by train from all corners of occupied Europe before calmly dispatching them for death in gas chambers. Germany had been one of the most advanced and sophisticated cultures of Europe, and yet it set about the systematic extermination of an entire race of humans.

The Holocaust and the failure of other states to act against it remains the most disturbing and awful single episode of the war—but there are other events, especially the development and use of atom bombs, that raise distressing questions about human behavior.

Why was Auschwitz never bombed?

The Allies were made aware of the mass slaughter of Jews in the death camps long before the end of the war. One member of the Polish government in exile in London committed suicide in despair at the weak response of the Allies when a report on the Holocaust was given to them. A proposal to bomb the transport approaches to Auschwitz, the major death camp, was made, but reasons were found for refusing to do so. The most charitable excuse for the lack of action was that the reality of what was happening was too monstrous to believe. It is also likely that the Allies were simply not interested in helping the Jews because there was no military advantage to be gained by doing so.

Survivors at Auschwitz, where a death camp operated close to a large work camp. In storerooms that had not been burned by the Germans, 836,255 women's dresses were found by Russian soldiers.

Dropping the atom bomb

The decision to use atom bombs on the cities of Hiroshima and Nagasaki remains the most controversial issue of World War II. Its power made it incapable of being confined to military targets. An atomic bomb was a frighteningly powerful way of massacring people—thousands died immediately from the blast or suffered injuries from burns or from radiation. It was argued at the time, and this is still the main argument in defense of what happened, that the use of the bomb saved the lives of Americans and their allies who would have died in large numbers attacking and conquering the Japanese mainland.

This argument is disputed by historians who point to the fact that Japan was very close to surrendering before the bombs were dropped, because the country was not militarily capable of continuing the war. The diehard Japanese militarists who wanted to carry on the fight would have been overruled, it is argued, especially if the bomb's awesome power was demonstrated on an uninhabited island.

Six months after the atomic bomb had been dropped on Hiroshima, roughly built shacks can be seen amid the ruins of a destroyed city.

The building of the Berlin Wall in 1961 divided the city into two parts and came to symbolize the Cold War that divided the post–World War II world. It was enthusiastically dismantled by civilians in November 1989.

An important aspect of the controversy is the motive of those who decided to use the new technology. The American chiefs-of-staff, the military leaders, were not consulted about the decision to use the new weapon, and some of them spoke out after the event and claimed it was not necessary. It seems likely that the decision to use the bomb was a political decision and that the wish to keep the USSR out of the Pacific war, and to demonstrate to that country the superior strength of the United States, was at least as important as military considerations. From this point of view, the dropping of the bomb is seen as an opening move in the Cold War.

55

The Cold War

World War II was a "hot" war in the sense that it was a stark and open struggle over the fate of Europe and Asia, fought by the world's most powerful countries. When it came to an end, it was succeeded by a new struggle which, because it did not result in an open war between the superpowers, was labeled the Cold War.

The Cold War, which lasted for almost 50 years, was the cause of many brutal wars in many parts of the world. It only came to an end with the reforms of Gorbachev and the breakup of the Soviet Union around 1990. The origins of this Cold War, and the origins of the post-Cold War world we now inhabit, lie in World War II.

The war made the United States and the USSR the undisputed superpowers of the world. It was the industrial power of these nations, and the astonishing capacity of the Soviet Union to absorb huge losses in human life, that ensured the Allied victories. Nations that had been very powerful before the war were either defeated and destroyed, like Germany and Japan, or like Great Britain and France, relegated to weaker positions. Both of the two new superpowers wanted to control the political and economic shape of the world that was

World War III was narrowly avoided in 1962 when the United States and the Soviet Union reached an agreement over the siting of missiles in Cuba and this Soviet freighter left Cuba, presumably with missiles on board.

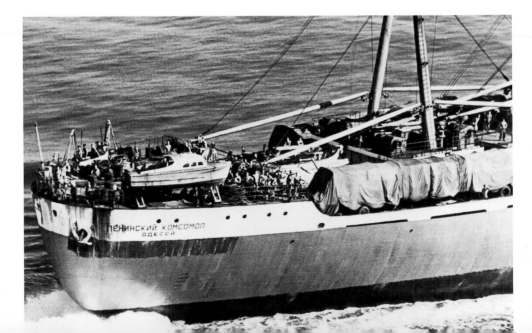

about to emerge from the ruins and rubble of the old one. Stalin's absolute priority was to make sure that Russia did not face the threat of another invasion from the West. Hitler's attack had come very close to succeeding. After World War I, the country had also been invaded by Great Britain and other Western armies hoping to topple the communist government that had taken power. In 1945, with Soviet armies occupying part of Germany and most of eastern Europe, Stalin was in an unchallengable position to build a defensive bloc that would isolate the Soviet Union from the West.

In a scene that looks as if it could belong to World War II, U.S. soldiers cover a road in Korea with a machine gun and a bazooka. The date is November 1950.

The United States, strongly supported by Great Britain, wanted to contain Soviet power as much as possible. The two nations did not want the countries they had liberated in Europe, nor Japan and Asia, to become communist, and they sought to build up a capitalist camp instead. This was understood by both sides, for as Stalin said: "This war is not as in the past; whoever occupies a territory also imposes on it his own social system. Everyone imposes his own system as far as his army can reach." This is indeed what happened, and the Cold War developed into a dangerous confrontation between two superpowers, both spending vast amounts of money on nuclear weapons and leading to a war in Korea in 1950, in which some four million people died.

A just war?

The rise of the new superpowers meant the fall of old empires and the emergence of new ones. It was the British Empire, so admired by Hitler, that suffered the most loss, and this was felt most keenly in Asia, where the myth of white superiority had been demolished by the Japanese in their blistering conquest of Malaya and Singapore. In Malaya, there had been mutinies by Asians in the British army and the British grew concerned about their rule in India, the most prized part of the Empire. They did in fact withdraw from India within two years, and from other parts of Asia in the years that followed. Great Britain was no longer a superpower and only recovered from what one of its economists called a "financial Dunkirk" (referring to the forced evacuation of British troops from France in 1944) after massive and costly loans. As Great Britain declined in power, its imperial role was gradually taken over by the United States.

In his memoirs, Churchill describes how he met with Stalin in October 1944 and scribbled down the names of East European countries on a piece of paper. Against each country he set a percentage for Western influence, a percentage for Soviet. There was 90 percent for Stalin in Romania, 75 percent for Bulgaria, 50 percent for Hungary, while Greece was to be left for the British. Stalin put a large checkmark next to the figures and handed the page back to Churchill.

Perhaps it never happened like this, but the truth behind the story is that the powerful victors in the war did, according to their own interests, decide the fate of smaller countries. In this sense, World War II was a power struggle fought for control of Europe and Asia, and not out of regard for the fate of the millions of people who suffered during those years.

Similar struggles for power lay behind the complex causes that gave rise to Nazism and Japanese expansion in the first place. What also remains true is that nothing worthy can be said about the aggressive and brutal policies pursued by Japan as the country expanded its territory into the Pacific. It is also true that the rule of Nazism was profoundly wicked and fighting for its overthrow was a noble cause.

Final homecoming for a soldier after the war is over.

Victory

Not in paradise, but on this vast tract of earth,
where at every step there is sorrow, sorrow, sorrow,
I awaited her, as one waits only when one loves,
I knew her as one knows only oneself,
I knew her in blood, in mud, in grief.
The hour struck.
The war ended.
I made my way home.
She came toward me, and we did not recognize each other.

Ilya Ehrenburg, May 9, 1945

Date list

<u>1941</u> *(from December)*

Dec. 7	Japan attacks U.S. base at Pearl Harbor.
Dec. 8	Japanese land in British Malaya.
Dec. 8	U.S. and Great Britain declare war on Japan.
Dec. 11	Hitler declares war on the United States

<u>1942</u>

Feb. 15	Singapore falls to Japan.
June 4	Battle of Midway begins.
June 9	Japanese conquest of the Philippines is complete.
June 25	Eisenhower arrives in London as commander of the U.S. forces in Europe.
Aug. 7	U.S. Marines land at Guadalcanal.
Aug. 9	Mahatma Gandhi is arrested in India after riots for independence.
Aug. 25	Battle of Stalingrad begins.
Nov. 8	Operation Torch: the Allied invasion of North Africa begins.
Nov. 19	Russian counterattack at Stalingrad. German troops are surrounded.

<u>1943</u>

Jan. 14	Roosevelt and Churchill meet at the Casablanca Conference.
Jan. 31	First German forces surrender at Stalingrad.
May 13	German and Italian troops surrender in North Africa.
July 5–12	Battle of Kursk.
July 10	Allied landing in Sicily by British and U.S. troops.
July 24–28	Allied air raids cause a firestorm in Hamburg.
July 30	Rommel assembles troops in northern Italy.
Sept. 3	Allied troops arrive on the Italian mainland. A secret deal is signed with the Allies in Sicily.
Sept. 8	Italy surrenders to the Allies.
Sept. 9	Allied troops arrive at Salerno, Italy.
Sept. 10	Germany occupies Rome.
Sept. 12	German paratroopers rescue Mussolini.
Oct. 13	Italy declares war on Germany.
Nov. 5	New offensives begin in the Solomons by U.S. troops.
Nov. 28	British assault on the eastern end of the Gustav Line.
Dec. 4	Roosevelt, Churchill, and Stalin meet at the Tehran Conference.

<u>1944</u>

Jan. 22	Allied troops land at Anzio.
Jan. 27	Leningrad siege is broken by the Russians.
Jan. 31	Marshall Islands are attacked by U.S. troops.
Feb.–March	Japan invades India, and is defeated at Imphal and Kohima.

Feb.–May	Battle of Monte Cassino.	**Feb. 13–14**	Allied bombing raid destroys Dresden.
May 6	Mahatma Gandhi is released from prison due to ill health.	**Feb. 23**	Stars and stripes are raised at Iwo Jima.
June 5	Allies enter and capture Rome.	**March 9**	Massive U.S. firebomb attack on Tokyo.
June 6	D-Day landings in Normandy.	**March 24**	Allies cross the Rhine.
June 17	Saipan in the Marianas Islands stormed by U.S. forces.	**April 1**	U.S. troops land on Okinawa.
June 20	Victory for the United States at the Battle of the Philippine Sea.	**April 22**	Russia launches final assault against Berlin.
June 22	Russian advance westward into Belarus —Operation Bagration.	**April 28**	Mussolini shot and hanged by Italian partisans.
June 27	U.S. troops capture Cherbourg.	**April 30**	Berlin falls to the Russians.
July 8	British and Canadian troops enter Caen.	**April 30**	Hitler commits suicide.
July 20	Assassination attempt on Hitler fails.	**May 7**	Germany surrenders unconditionally to the Allies in Rheims.
Aug.–Dec.	Russians sweep through Baltic states.	**May 8**	VE (Victory in Europe) Day.
Aug. 1	Warsaw uprising—a disaster for the Poles.	**June 21**	Okinawa taken by U.S. troops.
Aug. 10	U.S. conquest of Guam completed.	**July 17– Aug. 2**	Potsdam Conference, the final Allied summit.
Oct. 14	Rommel commits suicide.	**Aug. 6**	Atomic bomb dropped on Hiroshima, Japan.
Oct. 20	U.S. troops arrive in the Philippines.	**Aug. 9**	Russia declares war on Japan.
Oct. 24	Battle of Leyte Gulf.	**Aug. 9**	Atomic bomb dropped on Nagasaki, Japan.
Dec. 16–27	German counter-offensive in the Ardennes.	**Aug. 14**	Japan surrenders unconditionally to the Allies.
1945		**Aug. 15**	VJ (Victory over Japan) Day.
Jan. 17	Russians enter Warsaw.	**Sept. 2**	Japan formally surrenders in Tokyo Bay.
Jan. 24	Attack on Palembang oil targets, Indonesia.		

Glossary

aircraft carrier a large ship with a flying deck where aircraft can take off and land.

Allies the countries at war with Germany, Japan, and their supporters.

amphibious operating on both land and water.

atrocity an act of violence by an enemy armed force on civilians or prisoners.

Axis countries at war with the United States, Great Britain, and their allies.

battleship the largest and most heavily armed type of warship.

cease-fire a suspension of active hostilities, or a truce.

conscription compulsory enlistment of people for the purpose of conducting a war.

convoy a group of ships traveling together for safety.

D-Day short for Deliverance Day, the invasion of northern France by the Allies in June 1944.

death camps units for the systematic elimination of Jews by the Nazis during World War II.

division an army unit, with its own artillery, engineers, and so on, under a single command.

Fascism authoritarian government that started in Italy under Mussolini. It also describes Hitler's dictatorship in Germany.

Holocaust the systematic murder of Jews by Nazi Germany.

indoctrination instructed in practices or principles.

kamikaze Japanese suicide pilots undertaking missions against enemy ships.

Mustang a successful U.S. fighter plane that escorted B-17s and B-24s on missions over Germany. It was also used as a fighter-bomber.

Nazi a member of Hitler's National Socialist German Workers Party, which governed Germany between 1933 and 1945.

neutral not supporting or favoring one side over another in a war or dispute.

panzer the general term for a German tank or armored unit.

partisans guerrilla groups fighting the enemy in wartime.

pincer movement an encircling movement by two wings of an army, converging on the enemy.

RAF the Royal Air Force; the air force of Great Britain.

Red Army the name of the army of the USSR.

resistance group an underground organization struggling to achieve victory for a cause in a country under military occupation or an authoritarian government.

Sherman a reliable tank used more widely than any other Allied armored vehicle.

Suez Canal a waterway linking the Mediterranean and the Red Sea.

superpower a world power, such as the United States or the Soviet Union, that at the end of the war could exert influence over less powerful countries.

U-boat German submarine.

USAAF the U.S. Army Air Force formerly known as the USAAC, the U.S. Army Air Corps. After the war, it became the U.S. Air Force.

Sources and Resources

Further reading

Nicola Barber: *World War II*, Evans Brothers, 1994. A calendar of events of the war and how they affected people all over Europe.

Neil De Marco: *The Era of World War II*, OUP, 1993. Investigating history at Key Stage 3.

Colin Shepherd and Andy Reid: *Peace and War*, 1993. Pupil's book for the School's History Project's core text with emphasis on the causes of the war.

Also of interest

Stewart Binns and Adrian Wood: *World War II in Color*, Pavilion, 2000. This book is worth looking into for its wealth of color photographs.

Bob Carruthers and John Erickson: *The Russian Front 1941–1945*, Cassell, 1999. An illustrated book looking at the war between Nazi Germany and the Soviet Union.

Bob Carruthers and Simon Trew: *The Normandy Battles*, Cassell, 2000. A well-illustrated history of the battles in the decisive fight for Normandy.

Eric Lomax: *The Railway Man*, Vintage, 1996. Eric Lomax was taken prisoner after the fall of Singapore and sent to work on the Burma-Thailand railway. Fifty years later he discovers that one of his Japanese interrogators is still alive and sets out to meet him. An astonishing tale of bitterness and eventual forgiveness.

Laurence Rees: *War of the Century*, BBC, 1999. Another good overview of the war with plenty of illustrations.

A.J.P. Taylor: *World War II*, Penguin, 1975. A useful introduction to the military course of World War II; with lots of illustrations and maps.

Sources

Paul Fussell: *Wartime*, Oxford, 1989

Martin Kitchen: *A World in Flames,* Longman, 1990

Charles Messenger: *World War II in the West,* Cassell, 1999

Richard Overy: *Russia's War,* Penguin, 1998

Richard Overy: *Why the Allies Won,* Jonathan Cape, 1995

H.P. Willmott: *World War II in the East,* Cassell, 1999

Places to visit

The Imperial War Museum in London has various exhibitions relating to World War II and a shop selling posters, facsimile document packs, archive film videos, and other material suitable for projects that can be ordered from the museum.

Internet

Enter World War II in your search program for a list of possible sites. Two useful sites to find are:

The Imperial War Museum at: http://www.iwm.org.uk/

This site has online exhibitions, a mail order service, and links to other sites.

The BBC website also features World War II at:

http://www.bbc.co.uk/history/

Index